Come to the Party!

Celebrate Chinese Festivals

Suzanne Lauridsen   Sally Heinrich

Festivals tend to evolve as they
travel from place to place.
This book does not attempt to
portray the definitive versions
of Chinese festivals, but merely
describe how some of them
are celebrated in the
Asia-Pacific region.

Hello!
My name is Ping.
I am Chinese.
This is my friend, Max.
I am taking him to some Chinese festivals.
Come with us!

Chinese New Year

It is Chinese New Year's Eve. Max is helping us clean our house.

We always give our house a big clean especially for Chinese New Year — but never, ever on New Year's Day. My mum says that if you clean on New Year's Day, it sweeps away all the good luck for the whole year.

See the little kumquat tree outside our door? We have one every Chinese New Year. Its fruit is lucky because it looks like gold, the colour of wealth.

"Hurry up, Max!" I say.

We must finish our cleaning before the reunion dinner.

Max is a special guest at our family reunion dinner. All my cousins, uncles and aunties, grandmas and grandpas are here. Everyone is wearing nice new clothes.

"Wow! Your dress is as red as a fire engine," says Max.

The grown-ups give the children red paper packets with money inside them. They are called *hong bao.* Max gets some, too.

We are very excited because we're allowed to stay up late tonight. We believe that the later children stay up on New Year's Eve, the longer our parents will live.

Hong bao: A small red envelope containing a sum of money in an even-numbered amount, given by married couples to children and unmarried adults during Chinese New Year, and on other special occasions. It is also called *ang pow* and *lai see.*

We are in Chinatown on New Year's Day.

"I've never seen so much red in all my life!" says Max.

"There's a reason for that," I tell Max. "A long time ago, a little town in China was being bullied by a big monster. Every New Year, he came down from his mountain and ate a person or two.

"Then one year, somebody found out that this monster was scared of three things — the colour red, bright lights and loud noises.

"So the next New Year's Eve, everyone hung up bits of red paper and lit their lanterns. When the monster came, they banged on their pots and pans as loud as they could. The monster ran away and never came back!"

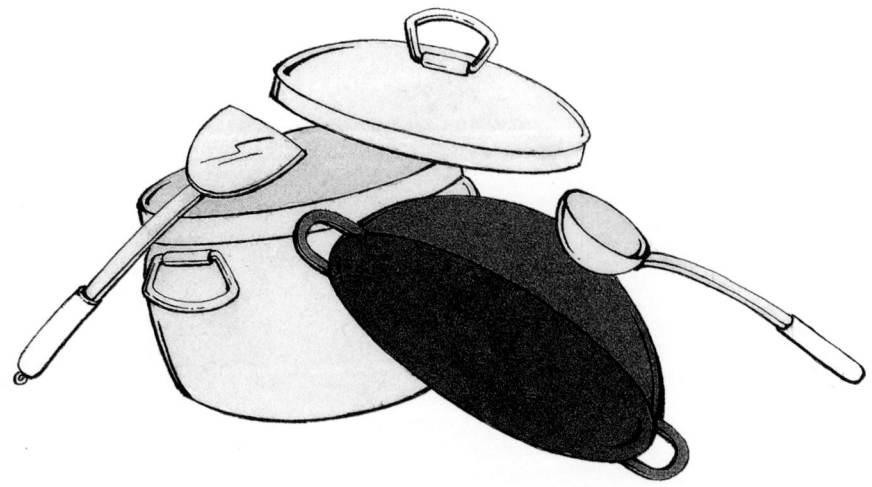

Chinatown: The part of a city where Chinese people live, shop and gather.

It is a few days after the start of the Chinese New Year. We celebrate our New Year for fifteen whole days.

"What's that noise?" asks Max.

"It's a lion dance!" I tell him.

Bang! Boom! Crash! The lion dances up and down the street to the noisy music.

The lion scares away monsters and bad spirits. I think it scares Max a little, too.

Dragon Boat Festival

Today is the Dragon Boat Festival. We are at the river to see the dragon boat races.

The boats are as long as buses. They have dragon-faces and tails of fire.

Bang! The race starts. A person in each boat beats on a drum to make the others row faster. It is very close...

"Come on, come on!" we cheer on our favourite boat.

Hooray! Our boat wins by a dragon's nostril-length.

After the races, everyone eats rice dumplings. We call them *zong zi*. I ask Max if he wants to hear a story.

"Sure!" he says with his mouth full of dumpling.

"Long ago in China there was a good man called Qu Yuan. Some bad men got into power and everyone suffered terribly. Qu Yuan was so sad he jumped into the river and drowned himself.

"Some fishermen looked for him in their boats. They beat on drums to scare away the river dragons. To stop the fish from eating Qu Yuan's body, they threw rice dumplings into the river. The greedy fish gobbled them up until they were so full they couldn't eat another bite.

"So every Dragon Boat Festival, we eat rice dumplings and remember good Qu Yuan."

Now Max wants another dumpling. He's as greedy as those fish!

Zong zi: Pyramid-shaped rice dumplings with a savoury or sweet filling, wrapped in bamboo or *pandan* leaves and tied with string.

Festival of the Hungry Ghosts

We are on our way home from school. The air is filled with smoke. Max looks frightened.

"Don't worry," I tell him. "It's just people burning paper hell notes for the ghosts."

Now Max looks really scared!

You see, it is the seventh month of the Chinese calendar. That is when the ghosts leave hell for a one-month holiday in our world. If they do not have a good time, they hang around to haunt us all year long.

Hell notes: Paper money that is believed to be the currency used by ghosts in the spirit world.

Oops! Max nearly puts his foot in a roast chicken. I tell him to watch his step.

There are some fruits and burning joss sticks on the footpath, too.

"Does this have anything to do with those ghosts?" asks Max nervously.

He's right, of course!

All this month, people put out offerings of good things for the ghosts to eat. After being shut away in hell all year, they are hungry for some real food.

That is why it is called the Festival of the Hungry Ghosts.

Joss sticks: Sweet-smelling incense sticks that are lit when prayers or gifts are offered to the gods.

We sit down and the concert begins. A man sings in a high voice and a band plays. My mum and I are taking Max to a concert put on especially for the ghosts.

There is a big stage on the corner of the street. Max heads for a chair in the front row.

"Stop! Don't sit there, Max!" I shout out just in time.

Phew, he could have sat on a ghost's lap! The first two rows are always reserved for the ghosts.

We sit down and the concert begins. A man sings in a high voice and a band plays loud music. It is called Chinese opera.

I just hope those ghosts are enjoying themselves...

Mid-Autumn Festival

Now it is the Mid-Autumn Festival. In China, the farmers harvest their crops. Then there is plenty of food and they can relax for a while.

It is also called the Mooncake Festival. The moon is at its biggest and brightest, and we eat mooncakes as a special treat.

Max takes a bite of his mooncake. I show him the golden egg yolk, like a little moon, inside it. Then I tell him a story my grandma once told me.

"A long time ago in China, there were some bad rulers. The people made a secret plan to get rid of them.

"They wrote notes to each other and cleverly hid them inside mooncakes. Their plan worked, and everyone was happy!"

The Mid-Autumn Festival is sometimes called the Lantern Festival, too. On our way to a lantern parade in the park, I tell Max another story.

"A long time ago, some people killed the favourite goose of the Emperor in heaven. He was so angry that he ordered his gods to set fire to the earth.

"Luckily, a good fairy overheard him. So she told everyone on earth to light their lanterns at the exact moment she knew the Emperor would be looking down.

"They did. And the Emperor was tricked. He thought the earth was on fire, but of course it was just the glow of the lanterns."

"What a *bright* idea!" says Max, quite pleased with his joke.

Look! There are our friends. We join the parade and hold our lanterns high.

I had lots of fun with Max.
I hope you did, too.

Calendar

The Chinese lunar calendar fixes its days by the cycles of the moon. As it changes from year to year, only approximate Western dates can be given.

Chinese New Year, on the first day of the Chinese lunar calendar, usually falls in late January or early February.

Dragon Boat Festival, on the fifth day of the fifth month of the Chinese lunar calendar, usually falls in June.

Festival of the Hungry Ghosts, in the seventh month of the Chinese lunar calendar, usually falls in August.

Mid-Autumn Festival, on the fifteenth day of the eighth month of the Chinese lunar calendar, usually falls in September.

Time Line

Hang a large long piece of paper on the wall, divided into twelve parts — one for each month of the year. Label the months. Then mark the major Chinese festivals as they occur throughout the year. You can mark other festivals too.

Suggested Activities

Make a Treasure Chest

Buy an assortment of Chinese items from Chinatown, e.g. red packets *(hong bao)*, joss sticks, paper fans, Chinese New Year decorations, chopsticks, a wok and so on. Put them in a cardboard box decorated with red paper and mark it 'treasure chest'.

Invite children to pick an item from the treasure chest. Ask them to identify the item. Hand the item around the group. Discuss and talk freely about any relevant subject that comes up.

Have a Conversation

1. Festivals — Name some that you celebrate. How do you celebrate them?

2. Spring cleaning — Do you do it? What sort of things do you do? (E.g. sweeping, dusting, washing, etc.)

3. Family reunions — Do you have them? When do you have them? How many cousins, aunts and uncles do you have? Draw your family tree.

4. Chinese food — What is your favourite Chinese food? How do you cook it? How do you eat it?

5. Dragon boat races — Have you seen them? What other kinds of races are there? (E.g. running races, car races, horse races, etc.)

6. Chinese opera — Have you heard it? What other kinds of music are there? (E.g. opera, jazz, folk music, classical music, rock 'n' roll music, etc.) What is your favourite kind of music?

Go on an Outing

Take a trip to Chinatown. Eat some Chinese food — use chopsticks if you can!

Put on a Play

Write and perform a simple play about the legend of Chinese New Year. Some children can take the part of the villagers, some can take the part of the monster, and others can take the part of the monster's victims.

You will need lots of pots and pans, red-coloured things and bright lights (torches).

Make a Red Packet (*hong bao*) for Chinese New Year

Materials: An A5 sheet of red paper. Scissors and glue. Gold paint pen or gold stickers (for decoration). Coins, notes or sweets for filling the packet.

Instructions: Fold the paper in half, then flatten out lengthwise so that the fold mark is showing in the middle. Cut away a narrow strip from the right outer edge to the middle, leaving the left half higher to form the flap of the envelope. On the right side, cut a small strip away from the side and the bottom half (approx. 1cm), so that the left side is wider and deeper. Fold in half. Fold the left overhanging outer and bottom edges over the right side. Tuck behind and glue to form a packet. Decorate the packet with a gold paint pen or sticker. You can write '*Gong Xi Fa Cai*' or 'Happy Chinese New Year' on it if you like. Fill the envelope with an even amount of money or sweets, then glue down the flap and give it to someone special!

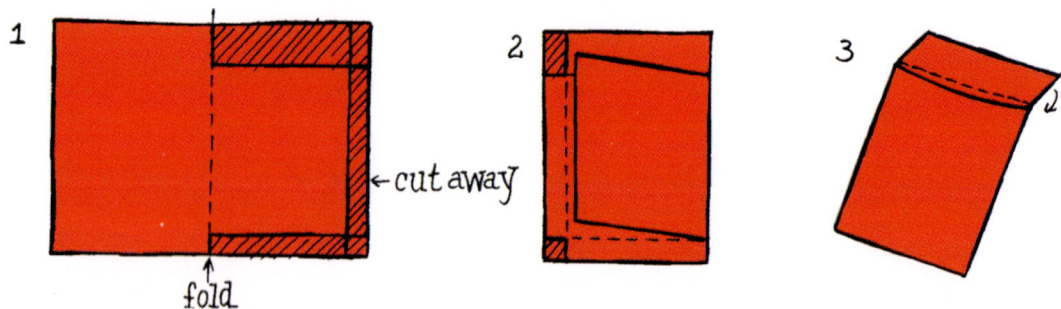

Make a Chinese Paper Lantern

Materials: A rectangular piece of coloured paper. Gold paint pen (for decoration). A narrow strip of paper (for handle). Glue and scissors.

Instructions: Fold the rectangular piece of paper in half lengthwise. Make cuts (straight or wavy) along the folded edge, ending approx. 2cm from the open edge. Open out the paper. Decorate the two long edges with a pretty pattern. Now bend the paper to make a cylinder and glue the two short edges together. Attach a narrow strip of paper as a handle.

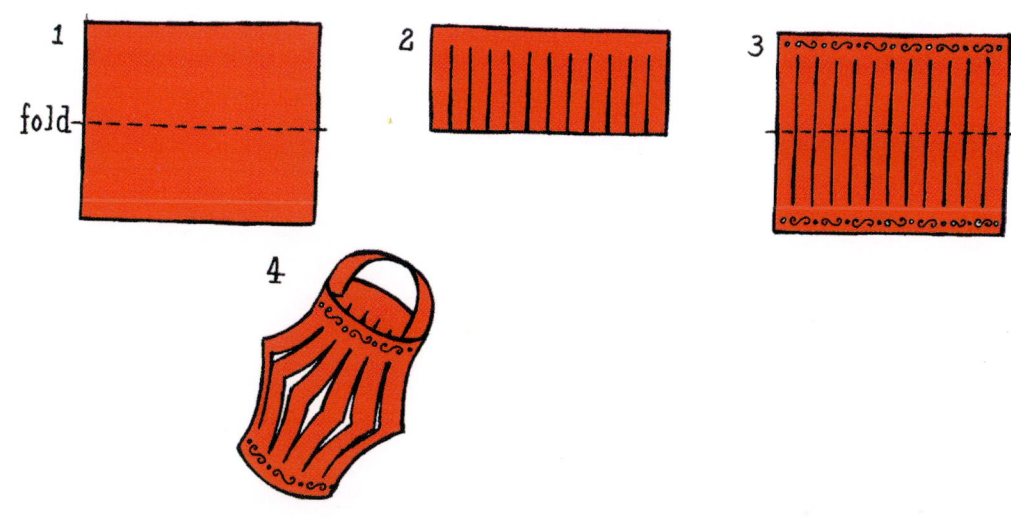

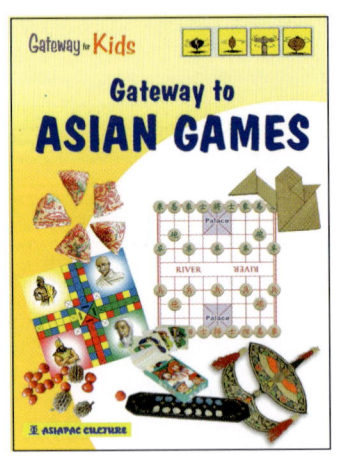

Gateway to Asian Games

From outdoor games like kite flying, rounders and hopscotch... to indoor games such as congkat, dayam and xiangqi, the book sheds light on Asia's history and the lives of your parents and grandparents. *150x210mm, 128pp, full colour, ISBN 981-229-445-7.*

Gateway to Singapore Culture

What do you know about the traditions of your own community, including our classmates and neighbours? Read and find out! *150x210mm, 96pp, full colour, ISBN 981-229-385-X.*

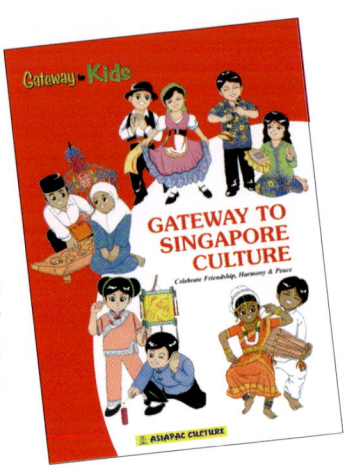

Publisher
ASIAPAC BOOKS PTE LTD
996 Bendemeer Road #06-09 Singapore 339944
Tel: (65) 63928455 Fax: (65) 63926455
Email asiapacbooks@pacific.net.sg

Come visit us at our Internet home page
www.asiapacbooks.com

This revised edition
First published December 2005
Reprinted November 2006

Printed in Singapore by FuIsland Offset Printing